Making My Dreams A Reality

by Kaleb Jarrod Porter

© 2024

Preface

This book was written to inspire myself and others to not be afraid to step out on dreams in life.

Dedication

This book is dedicated to anyone who is afraid of their dream not coming true. Push, pray, and pursue until something happens. To my parents and siblings, keep rising to the top. We're going to give it all we've got.

Have you ever heard an angel sing? I can. I want to become a famous singer so I can touch the lives of people. I believe singing is fun, because you can sing in front of a crowd and meet people.

The most important thing is to be brave when you sing. I believe you can't just get on a stage and sing a song. You need to put God first.

Instruments, such as keyboards, horns, and drums, make noise. Instruments can be big, medium, or small. Once you have your instrument from the store, you have what you need to begin your singing journey. You take the instrument so you can play it with the person that is singing. That's me. I'm the singer.

I believe my voice sounds good. I'm sure that your voice sounds good, too. But my voice doesn't always sound good. Sometimes, it sounds bad.

Microphones can help. Microphones are cool because when you speak into them, it amplifies your voice. Microphones help people to hear you when you sing. In my church, we use microphones so people can hear the singers and the preacher.

I want to be a famous singer one day. I think it might be fun. Singing is my dream. Right now, I sing at home and on a choir. Singing is a part of my life.

Some people say I sing good gospel songs. I can encourage others to step out on faith and sing their songs, also. Read Hebrews 12:1.

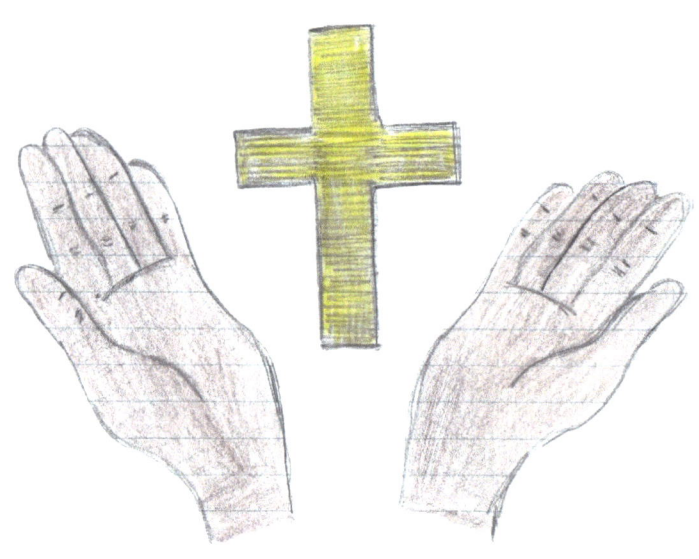

I enjoyed when my Aunt Londa would sing. I feel like I get my talent from her. She's an angel in Heaven that listens to me sing. Can you hear an angel sing, too?

My mother, sister, and my entire family inspires me to sing. I believe I need to be bold in what I want to do and encounter more from God as He lifts me up to do His will. I will always put God first in everything I do.
Read Philippians 3:16.

Sometimes, I have stage fright. Stage fright is when you get scared to sing in front of people. Even though I experience stage fright, I still want to follow my dream.

I want to sing and encourage others through songs and the way I live my life. Even if I must sing with my eyes closed, I will. I keep my mind and heart on my song.

My sister is very brave. She really inspired me when she sang at my uncle's funeral. She sang in front of a lot of people. Because of her, I know I don't have to be afraid.

I thank God for my family.

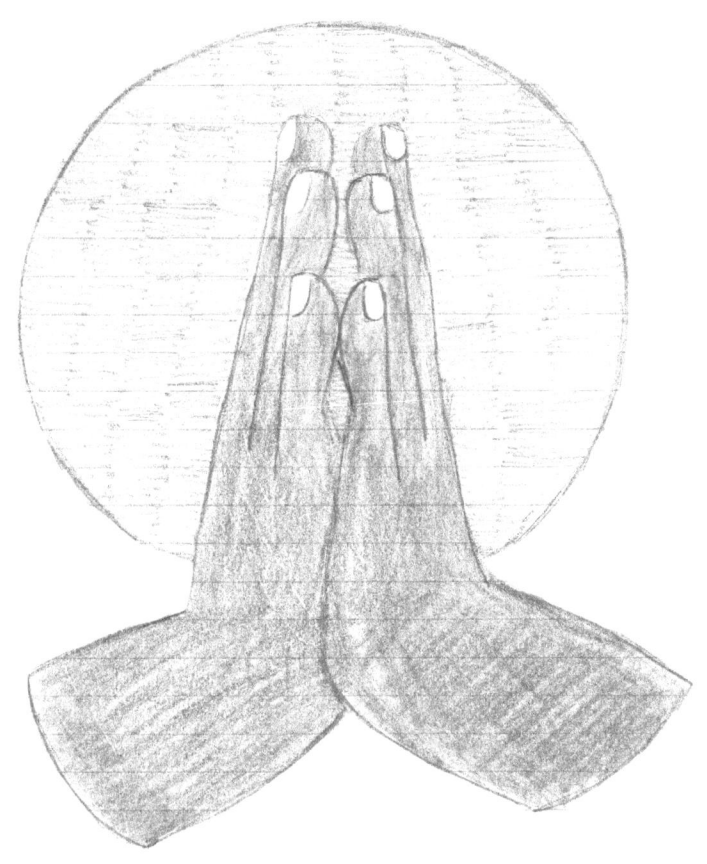

I thank God for giving me the idea to write a book to inspire young kids and adults to follow their dreams.

I pray that my book reaches millions of children and adults.

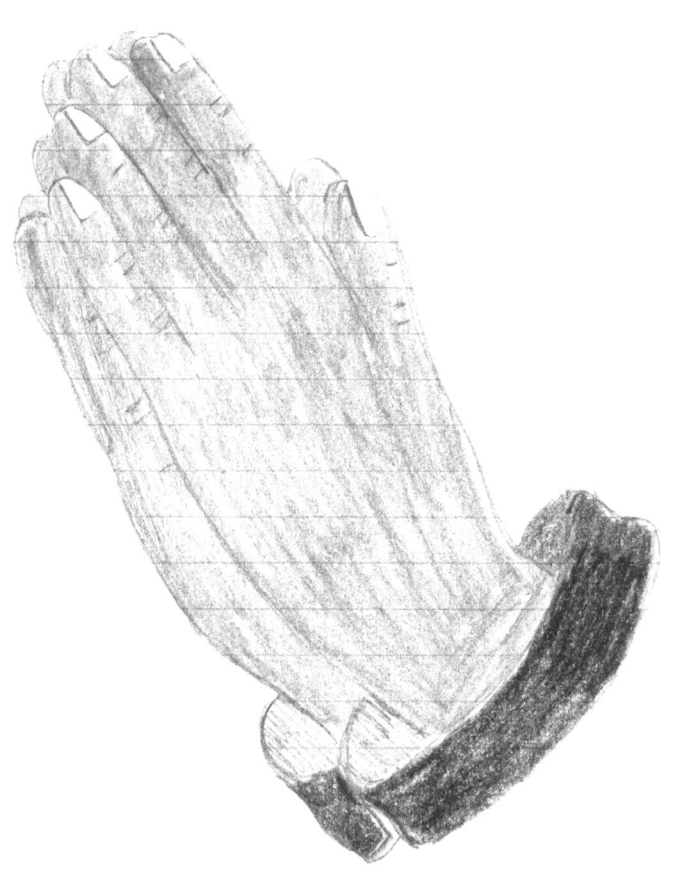

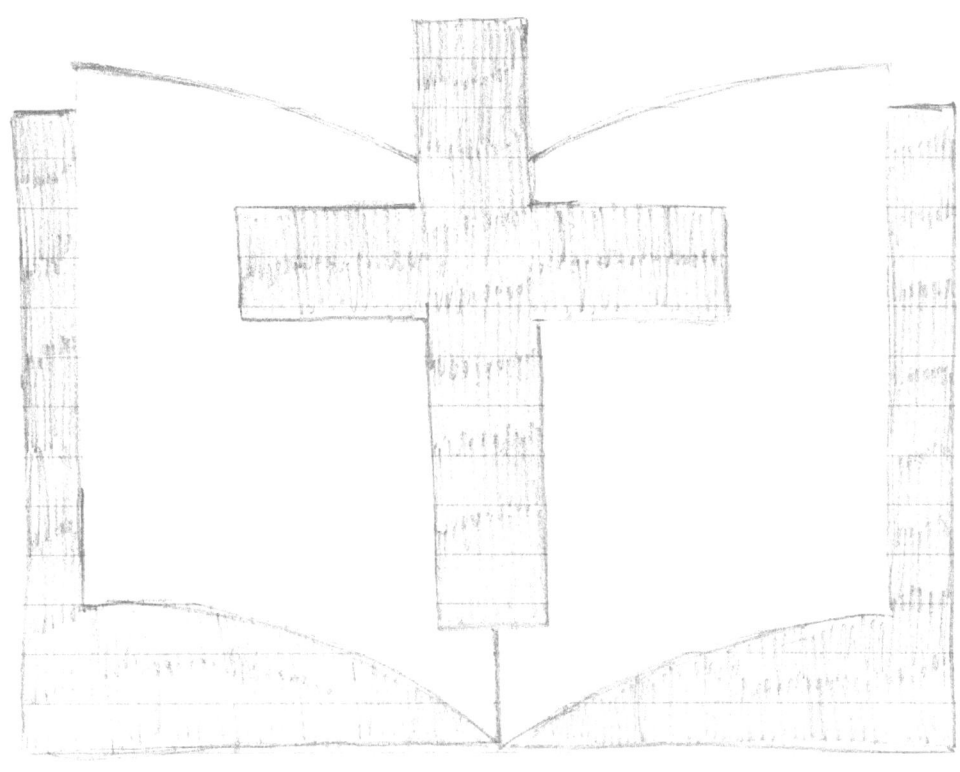

Here is my prayer:

Father, to everyone who reads my book, let it be a word to encourage them to follow their dreams.

We may be afraid or have doubt, but when we call on you, you step in at the right time and place. In Jesus' name. Amen.

My mom says words for thoughts like "Level Up."

"Elevate."

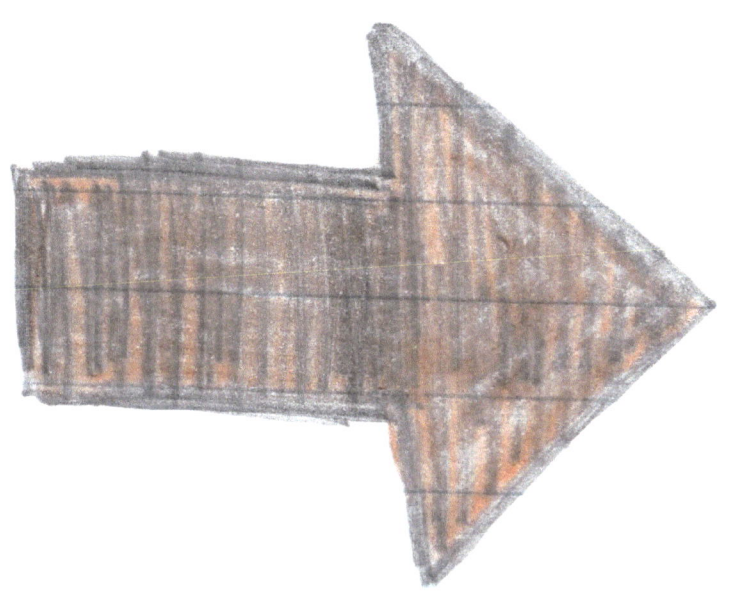

"To The Next."

"We Are Shifting To The Next."

This is my new saying:

"Kaleb."

www.ingramcontent.com/pod-product-compliance
Lightning Source LLC
LaVergne TN
LVHW010036070426
835507LV00006B/147